BEHIND THE BRAND

POKÉMON

BY BETSY RATHBURN

BLASTOFF! DISCOVERY

BELLWETHER MEDIA • MINNEAPOLIS, MN

Blastoff! Discovery launches a new mission: reading to learn. Filled with facts and features, each book offers you an exciting new world to explore!

BLASTOFF! UNIVERSE

BLASTOFF! Beginners — GRADE K

BLASTOFF! READERS — GRADES 1-3

BLASTOFF! DISCOVERY — GRADE 4

This edition first published in 2023 by Bellwether Media, Inc.

Library of Congress Cataloging-in-Publication Data

Names: Rathburn, Betsy, author.
Title: Pokémon / by Betsy Rathburn.
Description: Minneapolis, MN : Bellwether Media, 2023. | Series: Blastoff! discovery.
   Behind the brand | Includes bibliographical references and index. | Audience: Ages
   7-13 | Audience: Grades 4-6 | Summary: "Engaging images accompany
   information about Pokémon. The combination of high-interest subject matter and
   narrative text is intended for students in grades 3 through 8"– Provided by publisher.
Identifiers: LCCN 2022049476 (print) | LCCN 2022049477 (ebook) | ISBN
   9798886871449 (library binding) | ISBN 9798886872101 (paperback) |
   ISBN 9798886872705 (ebook)
Subjects: LCSH: Pokémon (Game)–Juvenile literature.
Classification: LCC GV1469.35.P63 R37 2023 (print) | LCC GV1469.35.P63
   (ebook) | DDC 794.8–dc23/eng/20221017
LC record available at https://lccn.loc.gov/2022049476
LC ebook record available at https://lccn.loc.gov/2022049477

Editor: Elizabeth Neuenfeldt   Designer: Andrea Schneider

Printed in the United States of America, North Mankato, MN.

TABLE OF
CONTENTS

POKÉMON IN THE PARK   4

GOTTA CATCH 'EM ALL!   6

ALWAYS EVOLVING   20

LEVELING UP   24

FAN FUN   26

GLOSSARY   30

TO LEARN MORE   31

INDEX   32

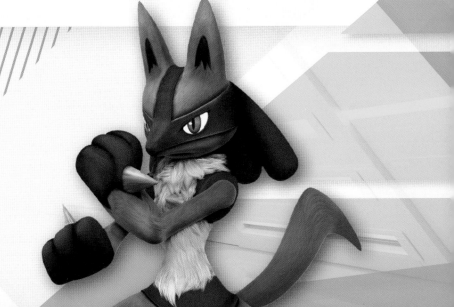

POKÉMON GO

A group of friends is exploring a park. They are playing *Pokémon GO*! They walk with their phones out, ready to capture nearby Pokémon. One friend spots an Eevee near the entrance to the park. They throw a Poké Ball to catch it. Another friend collects items from a gym. One of the items is an egg. It will hatch into a new Pokémon!

Later, the friends compare their Pokémon. They exchange an Oshawott and an Eevee. Now their Pokédexes are closer to complete. *Pokémon GO* is a fun part of the Pokémon **brand**!

EEVEE

OSHAWOTT

GOTTA CATCH 'EM ALL!

MERCHANDISE

POKÉMON
HEADQUARTERS

Pokémon is one of the world's most popular brands!
Three companies control the Pokémon brand. They
are Nintendo, Game Freak, and Creatures. Together,
they make up the Pokémon Company.

The company's **headquarters** is in Tokyo, Japan. But Pokémon is popular around the world. Since 1996, people have recognized Pokémon's **mascot**, Pikachu. Pikachu and the brand's many other characters have starred in video games, trading card games, movies, TV shows, and more. People can visit Pokémon stores, join **tournaments**, and collect **merchandise**. There are many ways for fans to catch their favorite Pokémon!

POKÉMON HEADQUARTERS

TOKYO, JAPAN

ASIA

Pokémon began with Satoshi Tajiri. As a child, Satoshi liked collecting insects. His interest even earned him the nickname Dr. Bug. Later, Satoshi became interested in video games. He created a video game magazine called *Game Freak*.

SATOSHI TAJIRI

BORN

August 28, 1965, in Tokyo, Japan

ROLE

Creator of Pokémon and founder of Game Freak

ACCOMPLISHMENTS

Created the idea for Pokémon and developed, directed, and produced many Pokémon games

NINTENDO ENTERTAINMENT
SYSTEM

KEN
SUGIMORI

The magazine caught the interest of Ken Sugimori. The two met and became friends. Together, they created a video game company. They named it Game Freak after Satoshi's magazine. Game Freak's first game was called *Mendel Palace*. It was released in Japan on the Nintendo Entertainment System in 1989.

GAME BOY

In 1989, Nintendo also released the Game Boy. This handheld **console** let players connect their devices with a cable and play together. The feature inspired Satoshi to create a new **role-playing game**. Thinking back to his childhood, he decided to develop a game where players could collect and trade insects.

Satoshi and Ken presented the idea to Nintendo. At first, the company did not like the idea. But Shigeru Miyamoto, a well-known Nintendo developer, believed in it. He decided to guide Satoshi and Ken as they created the game. Nintendo eventually agreed to help them make it.

MARIO'S MAKER

Shigeru Miyamoto has been involved in many of Nintendo's most successful games. He created Mario and worked on *Donkey Kong*, *The Legend of Zelda*, and many other games!

SHIGERU
MIYAMOTO

With Nintendo's approval, the team got to work. Ken drew the first 151 Pokémon. Each one had a type such as Water or Fire that affected its traits. Players began their game with Bulbasaur, Squirtle, or Charmander as their starter Pokémon. Then, they traveled the **fictional** world of Kanto. They used Poké Balls to collect new Pokémon for their Pokédexes. They also battled opposing players, collected items and **abilities**, and **evolved** their Pokémon into more powerful creatures.

BULBASAUR

POKÉMON RED

CHARMANDER

POKÉ BALLS

In 1996, the first Pokémon games were released in Japan. *Pokémon Red* and *Pokémon Green* were huge hits!

SOLD IN PAIRS

Pokémon games are usually released in pairs. Each game in a pair has a few unique Pokémon to catch. This encourages players to connect and trade with one another!

ASH KETCHUM IN THE *POKÉMON* CARTOON

POKÉMON TRADING CARDS

The Pokémon brand continued to grow. In 1996, the Pokémon Trading Card Game was released in Japan. Players could collect cards of their favorite Pokémon. They combined the Pokémon cards with trainer cards, energy cards, and more to hold Pokémon battles!

The Pokémon craze soon caught on outside of Japan. In 1998, *Pokémon Red* and *Pokémon Green* were released in the United States as *Pokémon Red* and *Pokémon Blue*. That same year, the *Pokémon* cartoon began airing in the United States. People loved watching Ash Ketchum on his journey to become a Pokémon master!

THE FIRST MOVIE

Pokémon: The First Movie was first released in Japan in 1998. It earned over $160 million worldwide and led to many other movie releases!

EARLY STARTER POKÉMON

Squirtle

Chikorita

POKÉMON *RED* AND *BLUE*

Year: 1998 (U.S.)
Console: Game Boy
Starter Pokémon:
Bulbasaur, Squirtle, Charizard

POKÉMON *GOLD* AND *SILVER*

Year: 2000 (U.S.)
Console: Game Boy Color
Starter Pokémon:
Cyndaquil, Totodile, Chikorita

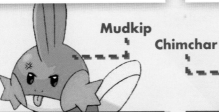

Mudkip

Chimchar

POKÉMON *RUBY* AND *SAPPHIRE*

Year: 2003 (U.S.)
Console: Game Boy Advance
Starter Pokémon:
Treecko, Torchic, Mudkip

POKÉMON *DIAMOND* AND *PEARL*

Year: 2007 (U.S.)
Console: Nintendo DS
Starter Pokémon:
Turtwig, Piplup, Chimchar

In 2000, *Pokémon Gold* and *Pokémon Silver* were released in the United States. These games brought a second **generation** of Pokémon to players. There were 100 new Pokémon to catch and evolve, including favorites such as Togepi, Umbreon, and Lugia. The games also added new Pokémon types. Dark and Steel Pokémon let players battle in new ways!

POKÉMON EVOLUTIONS

CHARMANDER	CHARMELEON	CHARIZARD
GIBLE	GABITE	GARCHOMP
FROAKIE	FROGADIER	GRENINJA
ROWLET	DARTRIX	DECIDUEYE

Three years later, *Pokémon Ruby* and *Pokémon Sapphire* were released in the United States for the Game Boy Advance. These were the first Pokémon games that let four players battle and trade at once!

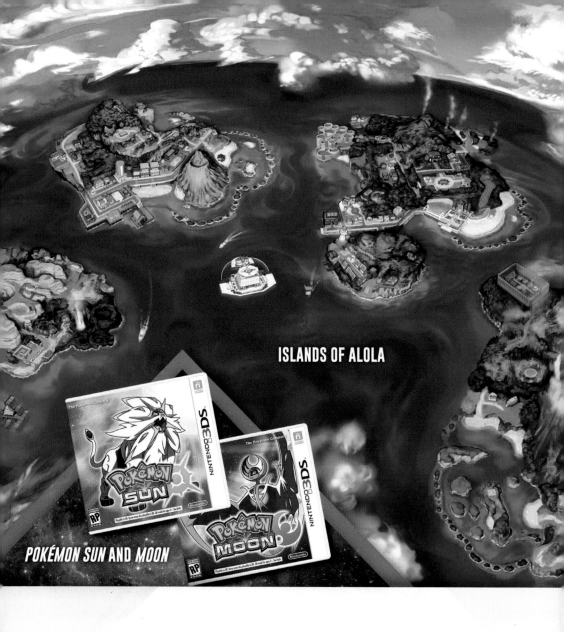

ISLANDS OF ALOLA

POKÉMON SUN AND MOON

More Pokémon games followed. By 2016, there were more than 800 Pokémon total. That year brought the release of the seventh generation of Pokémon with *Pokémon Sun* and *Pokémon Moon*. Nintendo 3DS players explored the islands of Alola alongside new Pokémon such as Rowlet and Litten!

The first Pokémon mobile game was also released in 2016. *Pokémon GO* used **augmented reality** to put Pokémon into the real world. Players could walk outside and use their phones to find, catch, and battle Pokémon. The game has been downloaded more than 1 billion times!

POKÉMON GO

ALWAYS EVOLVING

LET'S GO, EEVEE! ON THE NINTENDO SWITCH

DETECTIVE PIKACHU

In 2018, *Let's Go, Pikachu!* and *Let's Go, Eevee!* were released for the Nintendo Switch. Combined, both games sold nearly 15 million copies! The next year, *Pokémon Sword* and *Pokémon Shield* began Pokémon's eighth generation. Players could battle giant Pokémon using the Dynamax ability!

Pokémon continues outside of video games, too. In 2019, *Detective Pikachu* was the first **live-action** Pokémon movie. Viewers follow a Pokémon trainer as he solves a mystery alongside Pikachu. The two encounter many other popular Pokémon, including Bulbasaur, Greninja, and Mewtwo!

BASED ON...

The *Detective Pikachu* movie is based on a Nintendo 3DS game with the same name. Players worked with Pikachu to find clues and solve a mystery!

SALES SUCCESS

	YEAR (U.S.)	GAMES SOLD
POKÉMON RED AND *BLUE*	1998	31,380,000
POKÉMON RUBY AND *SAPPHIRE*	2003	16,220,000
POKÉMON X AND Y	2013	16,620,000
POKÉMON SUN AND *MOON*	2016	16,280,000
POKÉMON SWORD AND *SHIELD*	2019	24,500,000

The Pokémon brand continues to grow. In 2022, *Pokémon Scarlet* and *Pokémon Violet* were released. These were the first **open-world** Pokémon games in the main series. Players could freely explore the map and find Pokémon!

POKÉMON TIMELINE

1996
Pokémon Red and *Pokémon Green* are released in Japan

1998
Pokémon: The First Movie is released in Japan

2003
Pokémon Ruby and *Pokémon Sapphire* are released in the U.S.

2016
Pokémon GO is released for mobile devices

2019
Pokémon Sword and *Pokémon Shield* are released

1996
The Pokémon Trading Card Game is released in Japan

2000
Pokémon Gold and *Pokémon Silver* are released in the U.S.

2011
Pokémon Black and *Pokémon White* are released in the U.S.

2022
Pokémon Scarlet and *Pokémon Violet* are released

2019
Detective Pikachu hits theaters

Plans are also in the works for a live-action Pokémon
TV show. More **animated** Pokémon movies and TV
shows can be expected in the future, too. There are
even plans for a Pokémon theme park! Universal Studios
Japan will let fans interact with their favorite Pokémon in
a whole new way!

LEVELING UP

PLAY! POKÉMON
COMPETITION

The Pokémon brand works to make the world a better place. For years, Play! Pokémon competitions have awarded **scholarships** to winners. The company has also given millions of dollars to **charities** that improve lives around the world. In 2022, the Pokémon Company International promised to give $25 million over 5 years to help children!

The brand also knows how it affects the planet. Some people are concerned that the Pokémon Trading Card Game creates unnecessary waste. Some of the packaging cannot be easily recycled. The Pokémon Company continues to work to make its cards more Earth-friendly.

GIVING BACK

$25 MILLION
PLEDGED OVER 5 YEARS TO HELP CHILDREN IN 2022

$50 MILLION
GIVEN TO HELP CHILDREN FOLLOWING *POKÉMON GO* FEST IN 2020

$200,000
DONATED TO FIGHT RACISM IN 2020

$200,000
GIVEN TO HELP PEOPLE AFFECTED BY WAR IN 2022

FAN FUN

POKÉMON
CENTER STORE

VERY VALUABLE

The Pikachu Illustrator card is one
of the most valuable Pokémon
cards. It shows Pikachu holding a
paintbrush. In 2021, the card sold
for more than $5 million!

Fans celebrate the Pokémon brand in many ways! Many collect Pokémon trading cards. They search for the rarest and most valuable cards. Older cards can be worth a lot of money. Newer cards are also valuable. Each generation of games has new cards to collect. Card fans can even connect online. Card opening videos get millions of views on YouTube!

Other fans collect Pokémon figurines, plushies, and more. Some even travel to visit Pokémon Center stores. These stores offer fun items for fans to collect!

POKÉMON TRADING CARD COLLECTION

POKÉMON PLUSHIES

POKÉMON GO FEST

POKÉMON
TOURNAMENT

Pokémon GO hosts Community Days. People have a higher chance of finding specific Pokémon in certain places. The events draw crowds of fans. *Pokémon GO* Fest is another way to join in. Fans can meet, collect new items and Pokémon, and more!

Pokémon tournaments also draw big crowds. Fans of the Pokémon Trading Card Game gather to battle in Play! Pokémon events. Local Pokémon **leagues** let fans meet, battle, and trade cards in person. There is plenty of fun to be had with Pokémon!

POKÉMON GO FEST

WHAT IT IS

Yearly celebration of *Pokémon GO*

WHERE IT IS

First held in Chicago, Illinois; now held around the world

WHEN IT IS

Every year throughout the summer

ACTIVITIES

Meet other fans, learn more about *Pokémon GO*, collect new items, get news about updates

29

GLOSSARY

abilities—the skills or powers to do something

animated—produced by the creation of a series of drawings that are shown quickly, one after the other, to give the appearance of movement

augmented reality—a technology that uses cameras to place an image on top of the real-world surroundings

brand—a category of products all made by the same company

charities—organizations that help others in need

console—an electronic device mainly used for playing a video game

evolved—changed from one form into a new form

fictional—not real

generation—a group of objects or beings that are created or formed around the same time

headquarters—a company's main office

leagues—groups of people who gather to play a game

live-action—filmed using real actors

mascot—a character used as a symbol by a group or company

merchandise—items a company makes to sell

open-world—related to a type of game in which players are free to explore the game world without having to follow a story

role-playing game—a game in which players take on the roles of characters to complete the game

scholarships—money given to help people attend school

tournaments—competitions

TO LEARN MORE

AT THE LIBRARY

Dakin, Glenn, Shari Last, and Simon Beecroft. *Pokémon Ash's Atlas*. New York, N.Y.: DK Publishing, 2023.

London, Martha. *Pokémon*. Minnetonka, Minn.: Kaleidoscope Publishing, 2019.

Polinsky, Paige V. *Nintendo*. Minneapolis, Minn.: Bellwether Media, 2023.

ON THE WEB

FACTSURFER

Factsurfer.com gives you a safe, fun way to find more information.

1. Go to www.factsurfer.com.

2. Enter "Pokémon" into the search box and click Q.

3. Select your book cover to see a list of related content.

INDEX

augmented reality, 19

battle, 12, 14, 16, 17, 19, 20, 29

characters, 5, 7, 12, 13, 14, 16, 18, 20, 26

charities, 24

consoles, 9, 10, 17, 18, 20, 21

Creatures, 6

early starter Pokémon, 15

fans, 7, 23, 27, 28, 29

Game Freak (company), 6, 9

Game Freak (magazine), 8, 9

generations, 16, 18, 20, 27

giving back, 25

leagues, 29

merchandise, 6, 7, 27

Miyamoto, Shigeru, 11

movies, 7, 15, 20, 21, 23

Nintendo, 6, 9, 10, 11, 12

Pikachu, 7, 20, 21, 26

Play! Pokémon, 24, 29

Pokémon (cartoon), 14

Pokémon Center, 26, 27

Pokémon Company International, 24

Pokémon evolutions, 16

Pokémon GO, 4, 5, 19, 28

Pokémon GO Fest, 28, 29

Pokémon Trading Card Game, 7, 14, 25, 26, 27, 29

sales success, 21

Sugimori, Ken, 9, 11, 12

Tajiri, Satoshi, 8, 9, 10, 11

theme park, 23

timeline, 22

Tokyo, Japan, 7

tournaments, 7, 24, 28, 29

trade, 10, 13, 17, 29

TV shows, 7, 14, 23

types, 12, 16

video games, 4, 5, 7, 8, 9, 10, 11, 12, 13, 14, 16, 17, 18, 19, 20, 21, 22